Consciousness

My Personal Experience
Inside My Mother's Womb

Wanda Fonseca Serrano

Consciousness

My Personal Experience Inside My Mother's Womb

By

Wanda Serrano Fonseca

Serrano Publishing

Enfield, Connecticut

Copyright © Wanda Serrano Fonseca 2015 All rights reserved.

Serrano Publishing

Chapters

The Human Spirit Exists Before Birth

Abortion and Spirituality

Consciousness

Spiritual World Around Us

The Christian Perspective

My Spiritual Experiences

When does Consciousness Begins

Making Amends After Abortion

Dedications

This Book Is Dedicated To My Three Jewels; Ian, Xavier and Maximillian. May the Blessings of Abraham, Isaac and Jacob continually fall upon you.

And to my unborn daughter, April Spring, may you continue to enjoy the glory of the lord's presence. One day we will be together as a family and you will see your brothers as well.

Your Loving Mother.

Prelude

This is my personal experience in my mother's womb. Others have had the very same experience. This book provides my perspective as to why abortion is wrong. There is also a spiritual aspect of my life and beliefs and practices in other religions.

"I am a being of violent fire. I am purity God's desire."

St. Jermaine

The Human Spirit Exists Before Birth

What becomes of a woman who has seen herself inside her mother's womb as a fetus? Now and forever, I will be a spiritual being who is very much in touch with what goes on in the spiritual world around me. What I experienced as a fetus is far more symbolic than anything I have done for the past sixty years of my life.

As I made my way through this world filled with ideas and ideals about the meaning of life, I wonder how many people exist who have these vivid memories like I do. It was obvious to me that there were not many people who could have experienced what I had started to remember as the beginning of my own life. If there were more of these memories then no one would believe in abortion or the idea of ending the life of a fetus. What I can only describe as a spiritual experience, is the fundamental proof that life begins only weeks after the egg is fertilized and a fetus begins to grow.

I guess right about now would be a good time to say that I am one of the most humble and giving individual you will ever meet, and this is not an attempt to impose my ideals and beliefs on anyone but rather a simple girl's story of how this memory has affected me spiritually, emotionally, and mentally. But before we go to my birth which was quite eventful, it would be good to talk about the circumstances surrounding my birth. Although this might have some context as to why I am the way I am, I had to ask my parents about what transpired in order to write this book.

My parents met after my father completed his service with the Army serving in the Korean War. A Puerto Rican born man and woman fell in love and married. Thus, in the year 1955, on the American Island of Puerto Rico, my twin brother and I were born in the eleventh month. Yes, I am a twin. Shortly after, my mother became pregnant with my sister who was born in 1956, also in November.

After my sister was born, my father came to the United States to seek employment in the state of Connecticut. It took about seven months for him to finally find employment which prompted him to return to Puerto Rico after which we relocated to Connecticut. Moving to Connecticut was obviously an eventful process for my parents but it also was an eventful time for me. It would become a beautiful recollection, once my spiritual mind started to awaken as a child. I can recall a memory of me watching my parents in the apartment that my father had procured for my family. I can vividly recall my family congregating in the living room, and me looking at my parents, then looking at my brother and my sister. As I analyzed the scene in my mind, right then, I realized, "these must be my parents, my sister, and my brother." Once I accepted this reality, I got up and walked over to my siblings and began playing with them realizing they were the family that was provided for me to go through this life. While growing up, the bond between my sister and I was immeasurable. We were comparable to being twins. My mother unconsciously made sure we felt that way by dressing us in identical outfits every single chance she had. It is no wonder she became my best friend in my formative years. When my youngest sister was born eight years later, she joined the pack and became the baby sibling for us all.

The bond that our family had was something that developed as a result of my father's and mother's love for each other. Their love for each other, which I can only describe as spiritual, permeated our every waking moment. We felt it every step of the way, even in the ups and downs. Hence, that it was only inevitable that my siblings and I treated each other the same way. A middle-class environment, filled with love, and seasoned with the strength of my father, was enough to create wholesome beings out of my siblings and me.

I always saw my father as the perfect husband and provider, and my mother-the perfect housewife. She has the disposition of Mother Theresa of Calcutta. My parents never fought. My father was always a conscientious husband to my mother. He was always grateful and thankful to my mother for the daily meals she prepared. He worked very hard and moved up the ladder in his company, eventually becoming a department manager. This afforded my mother the opportunity to be a stay at home mom. Luckily for her, my mother never had to work outside the home and deal with the cruelties of the outside world. Up until this day I can still recall all the good memories we had growing up. It was easy for me to become who I am. I had zero trauma. It was easy for me to make the transition to the spiritual side of this life because of what was instilled in me from an early age.

Most people don't even remember those first moments of consciously recognizing their parents, much less their family as a unit. I consider myself one of the lucky ones.

Abortion and Spirituality

For many years now as a society we continue to struggle over the question of when does life begin. It is that fundamental question that has caused a split between most political, religious, and academic groups across the world. Every now and then I would pass by a Planned Parenthood rally and see a few people demonstrating against abortion.

Doctors have been murdered, women have been harassed at some of these clinics and yet, there hasn't been a clear timeline from any of the parties involved as to when life begins. I think no one will actually know the true timeline as to when life begins until God Himself comes down and tells us when that is. But until then, we are left here to surmise and decipher that fact based on our own personal experiences, belief systems and cultural upbringing. Whether it is during pregnancy or after birth, some individuals believe that life is meaningful and should be valued after the first trimester. Others believe life begins ten days after a fertile egg implants itself in the mother's womb, and there is a heartbeat.

For the majority of people who have formulated an opinion or idea on the subject, those ideas and opinions are intrinsically based on one's cultural upbringing or family systems. Therefore, the debate still continues as to whether the commencement of life is at conception or at the moment of birth.

I grew up in the Catholic Church, which opposes all forms of abortion including anything that would harm a fetus or an embryo. I appreciate the church's doctrine that is deeply rooted in the belief that human life should be protected at all cost.

My beliefs and morals became deeply aligned with my Catholic upbringings and still do up until this day. Being raised in a strict Orthodox Catholic home environment, our social life consisted mainly of the church, following the rituals, completing all the Sacraments, attending mass every Sunday, attending Holy days of obligation and praying daily with the Rosary as a family. Even today when visiting my parents and spending the night, my parents continue to pray the Rosary in the living room before retiring to bed and of course I join in.

A predominantly spiritual home environment, left me in a state of tranquility most of the time. This made it easy for me to mediate. My lifestyle became deeply spiritual, and on my own, I would take time alone in my bedroom, meditating and praying to the Lord, Mary and other Saints. Saint Bernadette was always my favorite. I love St. Bernadette because she was such a humble young girl and came from a humble family background. Her story is so beautiful and I fell more in love with the Virgin Mary/"The Immaculate Conception;" as she was introduced to Bernadette. Bernadette's story helped me to understand that visions from heaven do exist. Years later on December 12th, 1980, I had a beautiful vision of Bernadette along with four other holy beings. A beautiful, radiant, brilliance emanated from them. The first three figures were unrecognizable to me because they were blurry, and I could only see an outline of them. I was not able to tell whether they were male or female. The fourth one, who followed them, was less blurry and I was able to see that it was St. Teresa, the flower child of Jesus, as she is known. I was able to see St. Bernadette, so I asked her why I was not able to see all four figures next to her clearly. She said, "Wanda you cannot see them now, but you will soon. You must pray much, pray for the purification and the sanctification of your soul."

I can recall some spiritual things started happening to me. I was eleven years old when I experienced my first miracle. I was in my bed laying on my back when I looked up and saw a young angel suspended in the air in front of the bed praying. Although I sat there in awe for minutes, I did not feel any fear. I was immediately overcome by a sense of peace which I had never felt before. Suddenly, the angel disappeared and left me in an uproar. I jumped up immediately and started to look around for my sister, who shared a room with me, to inquire if she saw the angel. I realized that she was not present and heard my family talking to each other in the kitchen. I bolted down the stairs to tell everyone what I saw but found myself talking directly to my mother. My mother looked at me, smiled, and then said, "It sounds like you had a nice dream child." I tried to convince my mother that it was not a dream, but to no avail, so I just went back to my room, thanked my guardian angel and dedicated myself to continuing in prayer and serving the Lord.

The spiritual miracles kept coming. At the age of twelve I began to realize that I had a few spiritual gifts such as the gift of discerning, which enabled me to detect a person's true nature even minutes after I made contact with them. I would have dreams that would come true and would get premonitions that something terrible was going to happen even before it occurred. All of these events scared me, but I did not share them with anyone because I knew no one would believe me.

As I grew older, my yearning to be closer to the Lord grew deeper which lead me to want to become a priest. It wasn't long after, that I started sharing this love and desire with people, and was told that women were not allowed to become priests in the Catholic Church. The thought of not being able to serve God in that fashion left me completely devastated. It took a while but I recovered from that terrible news by becoming adamant about serving as a missionary nun and go to Africa to work with the poor. There would be other hurdles to go over other than the Catholic Church. When I shared my desires with my father he told me there was no way he was going to allow me to go that route with my life.

I started to assimilate into normal adolescent life while praying to God to direct me to a purpose-filled life. My world changed as I became older and stepped out of the confines of my safe home. All throughout this time I made sure that my constant challenges did not affect my desire for a divine inner lifestyle. It became more and more difficult to watch and learn the evil that existed in the world I lived in. I had no choice; my spiritual experiences and miracles would intensify and start to come in waves.

I experienced times where I would have an "out-of-body" experience, in which upon falling asleep at night, I felt my spirit leaving and "traveling" to other places. Although it would always scare me, I learned the signs of when my spirit was going to be on a journey because a heaviness would come over my body, and I would feel rushing wind blowing on my face. I could hear the wind passing through my ears and my head would arch back, then my spirit would be gone. Sometimes I would remain suspended in the air while dancing with what I recognized later as the Holy Spirit. One time I was traveling with the Virgin Mary over a small town in Puerto Rico called "La Montana Santa," translated in English as "The Holy Mountain." Years later I came to visit this town as I vacationed with two of my sons, who were toddlers at the time. My Godmother took me and my family there to visit the holy site in PR. Once I arrived and stood by the pond, my body began shaking uncontrollably. I felt the presence of the Holy Spirit there. At that moment, I could recall visiting this place with the Virgin Mary on a spiritual travel. I was in complete awe.

During the difficult times, especially relationships that were based in the world, and the latter part of my marriage, these spiritual experiences would become latent until I was able to extricate myself from the relationship. When I would deal with my significant others I would feel negative spirits rising up in them. These would battle against me until my spirit became weak and I couldn't handle the fight anymore. That was when I knew it was time to go.

"For we wrestle not against flesh and blood, but against principalities, against powers, against the rulers of the darkness of this world, against spiritual wickedness in high places; "Ephesians 6:12.

On one occasion while visiting my parents during college break, I fell into a deep spiritual sleep; another out-of-body experience. In my bedroom I saw before me the magnificent Archangel Michael and Satan, who looked quite majestic as well. They both looked at me, acknowledged me, then turned and faced each other, pulled out their swords and began fighting for my soul. I yelled and pleaded to them to stop fighting and they disappeared. I was not able to sleep for the rest of the evening. I shook all night praying for God's protection.

With God's merciful grace, I was saved through it all. My core is fundamentally defined by a spiritual development which has carried me through numerous trials and tribulations as an adult. I thank God for the spiritual foundation that my parents implemented in my life, especially my mother whom I see as a deep, spiritual, holy woman. I wish I was more like her. With that being said I believe it was my mother who provided the setting for me to become the way I am.

I can only assume that being a deeply, spiritual, Christian woman, my mother accepted her pregnancy as a gift from God. Referring back to the beginning of life. Hence, the path of the fetus in the mother's womb, will take on a definite defined development depending upon how the fetus is perceived by the carrier, i.e. the mother. Which itself is fundamentally linked to the mother's feelings and perception of her pregnancy during birth. That is the female either accepts her pregnancy as a blessing or she can see the embryo as dispensable depending upon the circumstances of her pregnancy.

Thus the question as to at what point does life begin is the foundation for the never-ending debate for the thousands of individuals who stand for the right to life versus pro-choice advocates.

Consciousness

My intentions in this book is neither to change nor convince anyone to change his/her point of view, regarding the right to life or freedom of choice, for each person must undergo his/her own personal spiritual path, and carry his/her personal spiritual responsibility in this current life.

On the contrary, my intention in this book is to hopefully help the individual who is genuinely searching for an answer regarding when life begins and more so, for those struggling with making the right decision regarding their pregnancy. Therefore, I want to share with you my own personal experience as it relates to the concept of consciousness, the presence of mind and spirit, which I personally experienced fully prior to my own birth.

Based on everything that I've experienced, I have formulated opinions that align themselves with the pro-life movement and even beyond that. I believe life exists even prior to the conception of life. This knowledge can be revealed to the fortunate individual, (in this case the woman), who is deeply in-tuned with her spirituality. I do think that a deeply spiritual man can receive spiritual knowledge as well regarding his prospective fatherhood.

During my academics I discovered Eastern Religions, in particular Buddhism. Being the spiritual being that I am,

I gravitated to the writings of Buddha and fell in love with the path of deep meditation and extrication from suffering. I fell deeper in love once I learned Buddha's teachings on deep commitment to Compassion and Forgiveness. It resonated with me and I cross referenced the teachings of Buddha and Jesus while he walked on this earth. I found a stark similarity in the principles relating to humility, giving to others, and always being mindful of your words, deeds and actions.

The Spiritual World Around Us

By the time I reached my early 20's, I had learned the art of meditation and began to meditate even deeper. I can easily meditate from one to two hours or more and feel completely at peace. Meditating or praying opens your spirit or soul to the higher plane and thus your spirit invites the spiritual entities, such as God, Jesus, angels, The Virgin Mary or other holy beings to intervene or interact with you through dreams and visions.

I believe it is God's choice to allow a fetus to be aware of its existence before birth, as God said to Jeremiah, "Before I formed you in your mother's womb, I knew you." Jeremiah 1:5. So therefore, I have to believe that we exist somewhere in heaven or in God's mind before we are conceived in a woman's womb. Most importantly, the infant (fetus) itself has full knowledge of his/her existence prior to birth.

I believe that most of us are unable to recall these memories because of the stress related to the birthing process. The problem is that the majority of human beings lose this memory through the process of labor for whatever reason, or perhaps subconsciously, chooses not to recall life before birth, due to the trauma process of labor and being forced out of the womb.

However, the fact of the matter is that CONSCIOUSNESS AND MEMORY EXIST BEFORE BIRTH. And, therefore, the SPIRIT IS ALIVE AND HAS

FULL KNOWLEDGE of his/her environment and one's own sense or essence of BEING.

I can assert this concept or thought because of one primary reason; I have always had perfect memory of my preexistence prior to my birth. Coupled with the fact that this preexistent memory has never faded from my mind, I can always bring this memory to the forefront whenever I choose to. What is even more phenomenal for me is that I can still see this memory crystal clear in my mind with all the emotional feelings attached to this period while I laid in my mother's womb.

Nine months after my mother and father got married in a Catholic church, she had both my brother and I. During her pregnancy my mother remained vigilantly spiritual and I'm sure my father did his best to make sure her stress levels were low throughout. My father helped her out in every way possible. In 1955 there were no such thing as an ultrasound, so when my mother gave birth she was very surprised to find out she was having twins. During the birthing process, my brother came immediately behind me and my mother's only recollection was that she had passed out in the hospital after she learned she had one more to push out.

After I came to understand and realize that this memory was an in vitro experience. I decided one day to give this memory my full attention and to analyze its significance. During my early adulthood, suddenly, like a bolt of lightning, its full significance and meaning unfolded itself to me. It was around the year 1993 during a morning meditation/praying hour when I suddenly became fully enlightened. I finally understood that I was fully conscious in my mother's womb.

I was driven with great exaltation and blissful joy to learn that I was truly conscious long before my mother gave birth to me. What gave my memory credence is the fact that part of this particular memory always entailed another being lying next to me which I had always perceived in my mind to be a little monkey. However, this monkey-looking baby was in reality my twin brother who also shared the same space in my mother's womb.

I shared my memory with my brother not long after I had that experience but he said he never had any memory of being in the womb. His words to me was that he thought my memory was "awesome." My brother is still alive and married to a wonderful beautiful Korean woman. They have a handsome son. My brother went on to have a successful life as a Chief Master Sergeant in the Air Force with the Medic Department. He is retired now and he and his lovely family reside in Illinois.

The following is a detailed description of what I experienced during the time of my mother's pregnancy prior to our birth. I can vividly recall residing in a dark environment not doing very much but just admiring my surroundings. From time to time I would look over to my right and would see this monkey-looking image. This being sometimes felt friendly to me, on other occasions it would scare me. However, for the most part it annoyed me and sometimes I wished it wasn't near me. As time went on I would take a deep breath and would think "I can't wait to get out of this darkness", "I'm so tired of being here. . . "I'm curious of this other being lying near me…"I wonder who is this being . . . ?" At other times I would just observe this being quietly. Invariably, for the most part I would lay in my mother's womb silently, just observing the darkness, or just patiently waiting for something to happen. My mind always felt vibrant and alive. It never seemed like I was resting, but rather I was just analyzing my relationship to this other being and analyzing my relationship with the surroundings. But for the most part I would lie quietly still. Just being in the present. Looking back in retrospect, it still remains a mystery to me that I did not recognize this being next to me as my brother. Perhaps it may have been that a part of my preexistent memory at that time was blocked spiritually for whatever reason.

I began writing this book approximately seventeen years ago, after my memory became crystal clear. Consequently, I would stop and start throughout as my personal circumstances would keep me from completing my writings. Looking back at my struggles I can see how Satan used many situations to keep me from writing this book. Finally in 2008, I had a vision of Saint Francisco and Saint Jacinta- the children/saints from Fatima, Portugal whom had multiple visits from the Virgin Mary Mother of Jesus. They encouraged me to complete the book and have it published. So I promised to do so.

I have studied Buddhism and the art of meditation and have come to some conclusions about their perception and beliefs about abortion. It is a religion that is also deeply against abortion. I say this to reiterate my point that most religions and belief systems in most cultures are deeply against this practice and that somehow it is linked to the beliefs of any positive force in this world.

According to Tibetan Buddhism, the mind is an ever presence, full of life and signifies a person's spirit. Tibetan Buddhism's conception of the mind is that it is the power of consciousness which controls one's persona. It teaches that in the end it is the mind which separates from the body and exists in full awareness or consciousness. It is further explained in "Zenatrophy," that "the mind of a sentient Being is not a product of biological processes, but something primordial which has existed since beginning of time . . ." Depending on Karma's path for a particular person, the individual either returns to earth by means of reincarnation or transcends to everlasting peace and tranquility known as Nirvana. Therefore, there is a break in that process when the act of abortion occurs. Buddhism seems to expect a moral responsibility from its believers that would not allow those individuals to accept this kind of behavior. Their philosophy which is written in their ancient text includes the connection of personal identity and the rebirth of life and death. Any reasoning or contemplation about abortion is referred to as carnal and self-serving. The only time it is not self-serving is when it is done by the mother to save her own life. But personally since Karma connection is there, then Karma is the one that dictates whether the mother should die in such a manner. When it comes to excuses for abortion it becomes a complex situation that cannot be easily deciphered by me or any of the philosophers of Buddhism.

The question that becomes clear for someone who believes in Buddhism and Karma is that of when the life of an spiritually advanced human being begins. It is quite obvious from my experience that embryos and fetuses are essential to life and development and thus can be developed into advanced human beings. If Buddhism accepts that babies are advanced human beings then it would be in align itself with anti- abortion which it is.

It is not like science does not back up consciousness before birth. It has been proven that the physiological development of an unborn child is far more advanced than what people believed years ago. In the first months of conception the fetus becomes sensitive to light and by five or six months the cerebral cortex becomes enabled for consciousness and can formulate distinct dreams.

What is even more amazing is that the child can detect the mood of the parents while in the womb. The unborn child can detect these feelings through hormones and neuro-hormones which can cross the placenta and affect him/her in many ways. Therefore, how a mother feels about her pregnancy can mentally affect the child. So it has been proven that there is consciousness long before birth because of the connection between a mother's feelings of love and the development of the fetus. This can wither if that type of stimulation is not met.

The Christian Perspective

From a Christian perspective, it seems to me therefore that the process of reincarnation can be viewed as a form of purgatory, the process of purification that takes place by means of needing to return to earth until one reaches the level of perfection. Or, the right to transcend permanently to a Holy state of consciousness.

On the contrary, reincarnation has never been taught from the Judeo-Christian perspective, which proposes that an individual only has one life to live and should you mess up, unfortunately you may end up either in an unholy state of consciousness such as in hell, which means that you made the conscious decision to separate yourself from having the personal connection with God. This luxury of Purgatory is only afforded to those who the Christian laws and rules but may have failed in part to follow the Ten Commandments. Their soul or spirit is given another chance and an allotted period of time to purify their spirit by spending time in a spiritual place called Purgatory, according to Catholicism.

Purgatory has been defined by many great Saints in the past decades as a real entity and by its descriptions, sounds as if it can also be a frightening place to be as well. On another level, Purgatory by others' description, appears similar to what I had experienced in my mother's womb. That is, the everlasting longing feeling to be done with such a stage of consciousness. Even during the state of Purgatory the soul appears to be fully conscious and maintains all the human emotions such as fear, worrisome, grief, and hopefulness in leaving Purgatory. In my mother's womb, I experienced multiple sensations, including the feeling of being ready to leave and wanting to enter into a new level of consciousness.

The same fact holds true prior to my pregnancy with all my three sons, including one miscarriage. Prior to each conception of my child I was given full knowledge of him to be in a form of a mystical vision far deeper than a regular dream state. This profound alter level of consciousness, that I cannot give a definition to, can be compared to an out of the body experience in which my spirit-soul interacted with another level of spiritual dimension. Perhaps my mind had extended to another level of consciousness defined by Tibetan Buddhism, as the third eye telepathic ability to receive future knowledge.

In any case, before I became pregnant with my first son, approximately six months to his conception I had fallen into a deep profound state of, what I believed to be at the time, an alternative state of consciousness or sleep. In the Charismatic churches, our belief system is that a person can be "slain by the Holy Spirit" without realizing it initially. In this alter level of consciousness I saw myself nine months pregnant on the operating table ready to give birth. I was experiencing labor pain while sweat was pouring down my face. Then a beautiful woman stood in front of me. Her presence changed the entire atmosphere and the surroundings felt as soft as a rose petal. She came closer to me and her eyes sparkled like two diamonds. Telepathically she spoke to me saying, "all those women who pray to me and offer their children to me, I will ease their pains of labor. . ." Then, she reached out her arms toward me to receive my child. I knew at that moment it was the Immaculate Virgin Mary who was in my presence and came to welcome my child to the world.

Like a bolt of lightning, I returned back to my normal level of consciousness. I laid on my bed, bewildered and tried to understand what had just happened, while at the same time trying to catch my breath. This vision I found to be so perplexing and disturbing at the same time because at this point in my life I did not understand its full significance. This was primarily because as a single woman in college I had no intentions of having any children any time soon. Therefore, I decided for a moment, to keep this spiritual experience to myself. In the interim, I gave my deepest reverence and thanksgiving to the Holy Mother for Her gracious visit, of which I felt I was not worthy by any means.

My Spiritual Experiences

Six months had passed and prior to the conception of my first son; I had another vision where I was given full knowledge of my child. I saw his face vividly and his coloring as well. He had light olive skin with dark hair. His features were fine, and I thought, "What a beautiful boy." Yet, I refused to believe that this vision had anything to do with me. I would minimize it as a pleasant dream.

However, the quality of this dream was so real and it would to a degree haunt me. Because it was not an ordinary dream. Consequently, these messages would come in as an alter state of consciousness that my whole mind and spirit would be completely involved and fully aware.

At age 25 I had no knowledge to compare these spiritual experiences to, so therefore, I decided to say nothing and began studying other religious denominations that would speak about alter states of consciousness. Due to the primary reason that if I referred to the religious teaching of Catholicism, and the Christian dogma, I did not fit into their mode of "Holiness." Thus, I began to ponder on the question of what constitutes holiness. Most importantly, who is right to judge what constitutes holiness? And does one have to be "holy" in order to have a spiritual experience?

After sixteen years of pondering these questions, I have come to the conclusion that the answer is "no." When it comes to consciousness and spirituality, only the Supreme Being God has the right to pass judgment, and decide to choose whomever He wants to enlighten and share a part of His conscious spiritual world through various forms. Hence, holiness is God's right to define. In addition to this, whatever mankind deems to be holiness may very well be off the mark from what God considers to be holiness. My understanding at this present time, is that holiness represents that person who has a complete conscious heart open to God and as well as the willingness or desire to want a relationship with Him despite their religious upbringing, cultural background, economic and /or marital status.

I also began to meditate on the Virgin Mary's position and the fact that she was only 14 years of age when she was impregnated by the Holy Spirit and brought our Savior into this world. In analyzing this situation I discovered that Mary was a single 14 year old teenager. The Virgin Mary was engaged to marry Joseph, but two thousand years ago the thought of an unwed female was probably unheard off, and most definitely forbidden. Mary would have been stoned or burned to death. However, the Guardian Angel saved her life by informing Joseph the importance of going through with the marriage contract due to the fact that the child The Virgin was carrying was holy and sent by God. God did not wait for Mary to be legally married to Joseph before God conceived her through the Holy Spirit.

God decided to make Mary a mother before she was a lawfully married woman. Therefore, God must not judge single mothers. But rather God can place His grace and favor upon a female or a woman who may become pregnant before marriage. I am not promoting premarital sex, or having children out of wedlock. However, every situation in which a child is born is unique and perhaps there were mitigating circumstances that had caused an unwed pregnancy. Society and nations at large have been very crude to young females and women who become pregnant before marriage. As if she got pregnant by herself.

This only occurs in a small percentage of women who choose in vitro fertilization. However, the majority did have a male partner, yet the male always escapes judgment and punishment, (either by society or from the family system). In any event, The Virgin Mary was pregnant before marriage and she is held in the highest celestial esteem by God. And we all must give her praise and honor because if it were not for Mary, we would not have been saved by her son Jesus Christ. Judgment belongs to the God Almighty Father only.

As with the first pregnancy, so were the succeeding pregnancies whereby I would receive full vision of what my child would look like as well as the gender to be. I was married at this time to the father of my three sons, whom I met going into my senior year in High School. I saw my second son with strawberry blond hair, fair skin, and almost identical features as my first son. My third son appeared to me showing cross features of the previous two sons. All three sons would call for me approximately four weeks prior to their birth. I would hear their sweet voices calling out "mommy", and then I knew I would be going into labor soon. No I am not hallucinating. It is an alter state of consciousness in which my children are letting me know that they are very much alive and are aware of me as much as I am aware of them.

Hence, should the question be posed to me as to whether or not abortion is either right or wrong, I would have to say most unequivocally YES.

Abortion is absolutely wrong because you are indeed terminating a fetus which has complete consciousness and the presence of mind. Whenever I reflect on my memory of residing in my mother's womb, I know for a fact that I was fully conscious and filled with the presence of mind. I felt I had full knowledge of my state of being and an awareness of my environment. And, I can only imagine that if my mother chose to abort me, my spirit would have gone into a state of panic.

At this moment I can only empathize with all those thousands of babies who had to suffer such devastation in their mother's womb when their consciousness abruptly ended, at least for that moment, for according to the theory of reincarnation, one's spirit returns perhaps to another human body or another family cultural system..

When Consciousness Begins?

The next question would be, "When does consciousness begin?" According to the reproductive cycle of the formation, the egg and the sperm coming together to create a human being, is instantly and constant until the fortieth week of gestation, so when the infant is ready to come into the world. In my case my sons were always ready to enter this world at the thirty sixth week of gestation.

Medical technology can demonstrate with the ultrasound equipment how the fetus' heart begins working on the tenth day of conception.

The heart sustains the essence of the human being. Therefore, it follows that consciousness must come into process on the tenth day as well. For if medical science dictates that life or consciousness has ended at the moment the heart stops working, and the individual is pronounced clinically dead, then one has to draw the conclusion that consciousness has left the individual's body. By the same concept if the heart is beating at the tenth day of conception, then life and the fetus' consciousness is very much alive and real.

Tibetan Buddhism believes that as a Master of deep meditation and one who has attained Samadhi, the monk is ready to transcend his mind or essence of being. That is to say that the monk's consciousness is believed to have transcended or left the body once the heart has stopped. In

Christianity we say that the spirit has left the body once the individual's heart has stopped beating and that person has taken his last breath. Hence, at the moment the fetus's heart begins to beat on the tenth day of conception, consciousness must be present in the embryo. Subsequently, we can conclude that on the tenth day human life begins and the tiny conscious being is highly vulnerable to the environment of the womb. So, for a woman to make a decision to terminate the growing fetus any time during the first trimester, (believing that the fetus is not worth anything and is not considered to be a "real human being"), or to believe that the embryo is not fully viable until the twelfth or fourteenth week of gestation, she is making the decision to end a conscious life.

In terms of a spontaneous miscarriage, what causes the fetus to withdraw from the mother's womb and be expelled from her body? The initial causal factor in most miscarriages is that the heart has stopped beating. There may have been other possible factors affecting the developing fetus, however, other malfunctions may not necessarily cause a miscarriage. For the reason that there are many infants born with multiple defects yet they have made it through birth with the heart still functioning. Thus, I believe that fetuses are miscarried when the heart stops and consciousness has left the body.

According to Tibetan Buddhism "Doctrine of the after breath", "The subtle is the human consciousness which temporarily ceases to function, there being in the case of the normal person, or of one who has not been logically developed before dying, a period of unconsciousness, lasting for about three to four days, immediately after the completion of the death-process. . . "When the deceased recovers consciousness, at the expiration of the period, he begins to feel at home in the Bardo, having passed through, while unconscious, the state preceding birth into the after-death world, which parallels the embryonic state preceding birth from the Bardo into the human world." (W.Y. Evans-Wentz, Tibetan Yoga pg.233).

Therefore, my understanding regarding this thought is that, the so called death state is temporary, and the conscious-spirit finds a new body or womb in which to be reborn while it is given another chance to reach perfection through the daily chore of human living. For the theory of reincarnation is to achieve a higher level of spiritual lifestyle on earth so that one does not have to continue returning to get it right spiritually.

In my third pregnancy right at the fulfillment of the first trimester, that is, on the twelfth week and going into my thirteenth week, my body began spotting lightly. This was strange for me, because the previous I never spotted during the two pregnancies. Although, my friends and co-workers tried to reassure me out of genuine concern that this was normal since others had similar experience, I was not convinced. And, although I tried to maintain an optimistic perspective on the situation, deep down in my gut I knew something was very wrong. Especially, recalling the recent dream I had when the doctors at the hospital tried to assure me that they did all that they could have done, however my "daughter" was too ill to make it.

My husband and I arrived at the ultrasound room and I was placed on the examining table to have the monitor placed on my stomach. It was the only time in all my experiences with pregnancy that the technician did not allow me to watch the monitor, or to listen to the wave sounds. Everything was very quiet. I tried very hard to read the technician's face, but she maintained a reserved expression. Although it appeared that she tried diligently to locate a heartbeat, finally the technician regretfully stated to me and to my husband that she was unable to find a heartbeat, and that there was no movement by the fetus. She quietly left the examining room to contact my doctor while I sobbed in my hands.

The heart sustains human consciousness. Without the function of the heart, consciousness ceases to exist.

Therefore, from the tenth day of the fetus' life the embryo is very much a vital human being.

Making Amends After Abortion

What to do then in the situation of a planned abortion? How does one reconcile the termination of a human life? According to Tibetan Buddhism, consciousness or life never ceases to exist. It continues revolving through other life cycles of embodiment, meaning that the spirit or soul enters into a new body until it has worked through all past karmas, sins, or wrong actions to prepare one's self to a higher degree of spirituality.

Hence, inner perfection or Nirvana; letting go of all carnal desires or "The state of Perfect Enlightenment", (The Doctrine of Nirvana; Tibetan Yoga and Secret Doctrines, W.Y.Evans – Wentz, pg. 7). Thus the life that was abruptly ended can continue to exist on another plain, or in another body. So one can believe from a Buddhist's perspective that the body can die, but the individual's soul or spirit continues to exist indefinitely on earth until it reaches perfection or "nirvana."

From a Christian perspective, life ends but the Spirit may continue to exist in Purgatory, heaven, or perhaps in hell. The individual's spirit does not return to earth to try again or amend his sins because it has only one chance and it is the chance we are aware of while we are alive or have consciousness. In reference to my conscious experience of being in my mother's womb, I currently have to perhaps consider the philosophy of reincarnation. For the reason that my spirit was very much alive, and I had full awareness or consciousness of myself and my environment. I know that I was not in a celestial environment, nor the burning fires of hell, thank goodness. Therefore, I must not have reached perfect mastery of myself or perfect spiritual sanctification because I was sitting in my mother's womb ready to return to earth.

On the other hand, from a Christian's perspective, I am simply a small soul that God gave an auspicious blessing to be given such an acute memory to recall my holy experience in my mother's womb before I was born. Praise be to God.

First, ask for forgiveness for having been involved in terminating the life of a fetus. The life continues to exist somewhere. Meditate on renewing your conscious spiritual connection with the spirit of the infant and ask the infant how you can make amends. Sooner or later, with a genuine heart, the spirit of the infant will communicate with you either through a spiritual dream, or a vision, and he/she will give you guidance as to how to reconstruct your past negative karma or sin.

I believe that we are living the best time since the existence of human beings, because today the majority of people are open-minded about new paradigms in philosophy and are willing to listen and ponder on new ideas and philosophies. I strongly believe that we should be open-minded as well where religion is concerned. I am proud to say that I was raised as an Orthodox Catholic. However, my spirituality has transcended to a higher level of faith and practice in which I have incorporated the fundamental ideology of Buddhism with Christianity.

For the last seven years I have been attending an Apostolic/Evangelical Church where praying for the blessings and presence of the Holy Spirit takes center stage. The year 2008 became a very tumultuous one for me and during that time the only thing I could think about was the need to feel the Holy Spirit in my life. I needed guidance and direction, and at the time, attending the Catholic Church was not fulfilling my needs. I so badly needed to feel God's presence to express my spiritual emotions in church which I was not able to in the Catholic Church. Yes, I know intellectually that the Holy Spirit is present in the Catholic Church especially during the blessing of the Holy Communion, but I needed more so I prayed that God would help me find a "Holy Spirit filled church." It did not matter to me what denomination it was, I just wanted to feel the presence of the Holy Spirit and to receive the Holy Spirit as the Disciples and Mary did in the Upper Room. I was in deep mourning about what to do and as I stared out of the widow from my dining room, I heard the voice of the spirit saying in Spanish "Pa Lante." I knew then to continue forward and the Holy Spirit gave me the strength to make major changes in my life once again.

I had been working as a Clinical Social Worker/therapist for the past 29 years and I obtained my Masters in Social Work in 1986 after I decided to do a field study as an undergraduate in one of the city hospitals to find out exactly what area of service I wanted to specialize in. I interned in the Pastoral Care Department just doing light volunteer work by sitting with medical patients. Across the hall from the Pastoral department was the Social Work Department so one day I walked over, introduced myself and learned all about the field of Social Work. It was then I knew without a doubt that this was what I wanted to specialize for my master's degree. I wanted very much to go into Hospice social work, to help the dying cross over, but ended up in Mental Health. I never had any regrets and learned how a tremendous amount of suffering exists among many families and individuals. I suddenly realized that the very thing I wanted to do as a teen was available to me right in the United States, and I did not have to go overseas to serve the poor and less fortunate. I started to talk to many clients who were suffering from poverty and mental health illnesses across many cities and towns in Connecticut.

There was a lot of poverty in the neighborhoods where I practiced. I also recognized that there were just as many ill people in the suburbs. The only differences in the suburbs was the fact that the individuals knew how to hide it or assimilate well. But mental health disorders such as depression, intense anxiety and substance abuse are rampant in all walks of life.

I perceive that a woman laboring with an acute crisis, some level of depression, or dealing with a deeply distressful life circumstances, when she believes that she can abort or terminate another human being, and not suffer great spiritual consequences from it. It is no different than if you decided you got tired of your five year old daughter or son and decided, "I don't have time for you in my life right now so I'm just going to stab you to death." I also believe that it is no different when the doctor is performing the abortion procedure and the mother carrying the fetus are stabbing the child to death together. This is clearly a violation of Exodus 20:13 which states that "Thou Shalt not commit murder," Exodus 20:13

As a Mental Health Therapist, I know that I need the protection and the grace from God to help do my job on a daily basis, for I work with very difficult cases and circumstances. One day a co-worker invited me to his church. After a few invitations I attended his church. Immediately upon stepping inside the church I felt The Holy Spirit's presence. When the Pastor was preaching I saw the lights of guardian angels present around the sanctuary. I knew then this would be my new church. I wanted to make sure that all my past sins were washed away and that I was reborn once again in the Holy Spirit. Thus the words of II Corinthians 5:17 always resonate with me. This verse says, "therefore if any man be in Christ, he is a new creature: old things are passed away, all things are become as new." Since then I have been baptized as Jesus was baptized. I was so immensely overjoyed to start my spiritual journey once again praying with the anointed gift of speaking in tongues in the presence of the Holy Spirit, Alleluia!

I am happy to have been praying to God to help me find a Spirit-filled church because my soul had been longing for a worship service where I can wholeheartedly sing praises to the Lord and receive the fullness and baptism of the Holy Spirit. The Catholic Church offers the Holy Communion each time it celebrates Mass/service, which, of course, is extremely important and vital for a Christian to receive the body and blood of Jesus Christ. It also teaches the gifts of the Holy Spirit. It seems that most Protestant/Pentecostal Denominations in this case, only celebrate Communion on the first Sunday of each month. However, it is equally important and necessary to receive the indwelling of the

Holy Spirit of Jesus Christ. I believe that both churches should find a way to merge since both have equal importance in facilitating the presence of the Lord in our lives, and I believe we need both the power of the Holy Spirit and the power of Holy Communion to be spiritually complete.

Since incorporating all three methods of spiritual practice; Catholicism, the meditation and the Pentecostal faith of praying in tongues I feel I have become so much more fulfilling and spiritually grounded. The Creator Father; Jehovah-Jira is the God of all, and we perform a greater service to society if we demonstrate genuine respect for each other's denomination and religious beliefs. Adopting and utilizing those ideas from all perspectives would make the best sense for all in achieving a better understanding of spirituality. Adopting the best practice to increase our faith can help us along the lines of purification and the right to receive Heaven. As a devout Christian I know that Jesus is my Savior and the path to eternal life.

Meditation

As a professional counselor, it is important for me to educate women about the monumental importance of caring for oneself during pregnancy. It is extremely important to be mindful of the presence of the fetus. The more spiritual one is, the higher the chances that one will have a good pregnancy and a healthy baby.

It has been theorized that a fetus can respond to sounds outside the mother's womb.

Furthermore, if you speak to the fetus during the pregnancy, the baby is surely to respond to the sound of your voice after birth. I say with utmost importance that by mastering the art of meditation. One can begin spiritually cleansing herself of a spontaneous miscarriage, or an abortion through the art of meditation.

So here are some simple ways of meditation. First, begin meditating five minutes each day until you can increase the time of meditation. When you have mastered the art of sitting still and going within, you will eventually be able to happily meditate for up to an hour. However, keep in mind that meditation requires consistent commitment each day or at least three to four times a week. Mastering the basic processes is dependent on one's ability to meditate and can take up to a year. The good news is that at the end of the year you will feel a new relationship with a higher spiritual dimension. So do not give up!

The best time to begin meditating is at early dawn between 4:00 and 5:00 am, then at 12 noon, and then at 7:00 pm. These times are connected to the most universal hour of spirituality and holds religious significance which I will forego mentioning until later in this text. However, if for whatever reason these times for meditation are not available to you, then it is entirely acceptable to choose another hour whereby you will not be interrupted. Also should you be a light sleeper and wake up in the middle of the night, go ahead and meditate then. Sometimes you will find that 3:00 am can be of great benefit to begin your daily meditation. Frequently I will meditate at any time between 3:00 and 5:00 am, and I have found that these are perhaps the holiest hours of the day. Do not force yourself to get up for the reason that proper connection to spiritual meditation is the desire of the heart to want to connect with the higher being. So if the desire is not there, then your meditation will be futile. The concept applies to praying as well. If you are rambling along memorized prayers, and your heart is barely in tune, then you may be wasting your time. You must feel the prayer in order to see any effects.

For those of you who find meditation to be a foreign concept, take heart. For meditation is a form of praying, only in a more profound method. Moreover, in meditation you pray with your whole conscious being. Whereas in the familiar praying method, most individuals are praying from the memory of reciting prayers.

Now in terms of pregnancy, visualize yourself sitting in a natural environment surrounded by beautiful greenery, perhaps near a pond or on a hillside overlooking a majestic pasture. Beyond the landscape, visualize the great sun sparkling with radiant rays. See the rays moving towards you, penetrating into your pores and mind. In front of the sun visualize a great being, which can be the Immaculate Mary, Jesus, a favorite Saint, or an Archangel. You may use any important Celestial Being which constitute holiness and one who can intervene on your behalf. Breath in slowly visualizing the sun's rays healing any pain you may feel. In addition to this, visualize the rays purifying your fetus. As you begin to breathe in, hold your breath for at least ten seconds or more if you can, then let your breath leave your nostrils or mouth, as you visualize all toxic waste leaving your body.

Do this exercise as many times as you feel it necessary to be cleansed. Thereafter, pray from your heart to the Holy Being. Make your request and supplication known. Understand that the sun is an extension of God's being. Remember that He created all natural materials and thus the sun is an extension of His Love. You can also visualize Jesus or Mary standing before you. If you want forgiveness, then visualize Jesus or Jehovah. After your supplication, focus your conscious attention or energy toward the fetus and engage in loving words with the child. Imagine stroking the head and holding the hand for example. Words are energy vibrations which go forward to the destination you direct them to. Most importantly, it is in the spiritual realm that your child can receive your loving words and have full understanding. When you feel like you have bonded sufficiently with your fetus, you can end your meditation with a traditional prayer such as the Our Father, or another prayer. Always keep in mind the necessity of feeling the words of prayer.

In regards to making amends for an abortion, begin the meditation process in the same manner as above. Visualize a beautiful scenery, see the sun, and see the Celestial Being. In this particular instance try to imagine what the Creator God would look like. Some helpful hints include visualizing an outline of a body form. See the form almost as an invisible spirit all in white radiant rays. The more focus your mind's eyes can see, the more radiant the Being becomes, to the point of sharpness as a brilliant diamond emanating fiery rays throughout. In the presence of the Creator, feel His infinite love pulsating through the multiple rays, enveloping your being. Know Him as your personal friend and allow your heart to ask for forgiveness, then feel the loving rays warming you, accepting your request. Know that it is done. Stay with this moment as long as you please, then end this phase with a prayer, expressing gratitude to the Creator.

You can either go into the next process of mediating on the aborted child, or you can come back at a later time to spend time with the child. In either case, transfer your thoughts or consciousness to the spirit of your infant and ask for forgiveness. Afterwards, begin to develop a spiritual relationship with the infant to gain eternal happiness as well. Pray that the infant resides in celestial peace.

Pregnancy is the most holy state of being for a woman because the Spirit of God is in her womb at all times creating a new being. Therefore, the state of pregnancy is always a holy event regardless of the woman's marital status. Suffice it to say that an unwed single woman or young lady is experiencing a holy state of affair as well, and no one has the right to pass judgment on her. Remember that she carries the Spirit of God throughout pregnancy.

As I stated earlier in this text, when the Creator chose the Virgin Mary to carry His Son, Mary was an unwed single young lady at the time. However, God found favor in her. God did not say to Mary that she had to be married and needed to hold a particular status in life before He requested her heart through St. Gabriel, the Archangel, to bare His Son. And, it was only after several weeks of pregnancy that Mary thereafter became the wife of Joseph. Therefore, single, unwed mothers should not be cruelly judged. No one knows their circumstances.

Unfortunately, in society today many women are being left alone for whatever reason to bare children. The best circumstance for most women is to be married of course, in order to have the husband partake in the pregnancy process. Unfortunately, domestic violence is prevalent in family systems today and in such a case the woman may be better off separating herself from a violent relationship. Whatever the case may be, the fact remains that the unborn child maintains his or her status in the mother's womb of being in a holy state of consciousness. Oblivious to the outside world, or the material world, the fetus is a conscious being residing in a holy presence, full of awareness, having the mental capacity right from its conception, and patiently waits to enter into this world. A pregnant woman should always receive the utmost respect at all times. It is a woman that allowed you to come into this life and gave birth to your being, as she made the conscious decision to choose life for you versus abortion. Respect her and give her honor.

I had the auspicious honor of experiencing a great vision with the Lord in which He showed me that God is an all immensely Love energy. The Love energy is so immense it is indescribable. He is through and through from beginning to the end all and powerfully pure love and not one part of His Being is less than the magnitude of love vibration. Lightning energy ensues from Him with Compassionate Love. I was immersed in his engulfing love. His voice said "Blessed are the pure in heart for they shall see God". In my vision I did not want to leave His side. I reached out to touch His energy and I was filled with indescribable Compassion and Love. God is Pure Love, and every child that is conceived is created with the same pure energy love from God, because God gave this gift to men and women to create love in a new being. May God bless you and your unborn child.

Amen Amen

www.ingramcontent.com/pod-product-compliance
Lightning Source LLC
LaVergne TN
LVHW051157080426
835508LV00021B/2677